HIDDEN JEWELS

*The Wildlife of Leatherhead
and Fetcham*

HIDDEN JEWELS

The Wildlife of Leatherhead and Fetcham

JEREMY EARLY

This book is dedicated to my parents,
Gerald and Joan Early

First published 1997
by Jeremy P. Early
16 Bridge Court, Bridge Street, Leatherhead, Surrey KT22 8BW

ISBN 0 9530098 0 7

Designed by Neil Randon

Contents

Foreword

I am delighted to welcome this book, which I see as a gift from the author initially to the people of Mole Valley and then to a much wider audience as well. I applaud his selecting a small area, studying it intensively and presenting it as a cameo which, of course, contains all the elements found in a wider canvas.

Jeremy Early has a passion for nature and for this place, and his book will certainly raise the level of awareness and contribute both to the enjoyment and the safe-keeping of a special environment. The Mill Pond in Fetcham and the stretch of the River Mole described are not in the wilds but in an area where 18,000 people live, and as such they have a particular attraction.

I read slowly, savouring both the photographs and the text and listening to a friendly voice revealing new aspects of somewhere already known to me. But this is also a book for newcomers to discover and appreciate what is here.

It is refreshing that the environmental message is not 'gloom and doom'. There is a balance. The facts are stated as they are. Improvements and the "sterling work" of the National Rivers Authority (now Environment Agency) are acknowledged. There is a positive expression of hope that, by taking care, we can conserve.

There is no complacency, however. We are urged to be vigilant, to be aware of the effect of strategic policies on our environment and, most importantly, to realise how we as individuals can enhance or despoil our inheritance.

These 'hidden jewels' are in our hands and I believe that this book will achieve the greater understanding for which its author aims.

Kit Oliver
Vice-Chairman, Mole Valley District Council

Introduction

Surrey has a habit of being underappreciated. No-one would dispute the glories of the Lake District, the Peak District, Dartmoor, the Brecon Beacons, the Highlands or the Cotswolds, yet how many residents of the UK would give more than a passing thought to Surrey as an area of scenic beauty or grandeur? Surely it is a Home County, just an extension of London? Surely around half the total area is urbanised, and crowded with commuters, cars and retail villages? Surely the M25, the M23 and heaven knows how many other trunk roads course through its veins? Surely on top of that, and increasing the levels of noise and fumes, there are two massive airports nearby at Heathrow and Gatwick?

Answering 'yes' to all these is hardly an effective riposte to the doubters, but the following truths ought to help create a better perspective. Surrey has a greater number of trees per hectare than any other county, including 16,000 hectares (40,000 acres) of deciduous woodland. Surrey has two of Britain's finest manmade heathlands – an increasingly scarce habitat – in Thursley and Chobham Common National Nature Reserves. Surrey has a substantial portion of the North Downs, officially an Area of Outstanding Natural Beauty, and in Leith Hill it boasts the highest point in south-east England.

If this defence smacks of being 'native', perhaps that is only to be expected. I was born in Redhill, spent the first 11 years of my life in Woodmansterne and the next 15 in Reigate. After a seven-year spell in West Yorkshire, Leatherhead has been my base for nearly 10 years. Surrey and its nature have come under my scrutiny in a way no other county can match. This has tended to confirm that intensive study of one area is altogether more satisfying and useful than hopping around the country, fun as that is. Living in Leatherhead has carried the process of concentration one step further without, I hope, giving rise to any suspicion of parochialism, for no wild habitat should ever be regarded in isolation. All are links in longer chains, and ideally local studies should sharpen one's concern for the natural world on a wider scale. Difficulties on the doorstep often represent national, or even international, ones in miniature.

Many of Surrey's treasures are, above everything else, homely, and while not always easy to find they are easy to appreciate. A kingfisher flashing past rich green reeds. Golden-leaved oaks above a well-frosted hedge. A heron patiently hunting on the edge of a pond. Roe deer browsing near a copse at dusk.

Leatherhead offers all these delights and much more besides. On the face of it, the geographical area covered by this book is small, consisting of the River Mole and its corridor – an average of 50 metres either side – for the four kilometres from Young Street (A246) in the south to Fetcham Splash in the north, plus Fetcham Mill Pond and the land surrounding it to the west of Leatherhead. But, in keeping with the 'chain' principle outlined above, although the main focus is specific and local, its application is broad. Just about all the wildlife of Leatherhead and Fetcham can be found elsewhere on the Mole or in its catchment.

The quality of that wildlife inspired the writing of Hidden Jewels. The hope that spreading the word about the quality might increase awareness, understanding and enjoyment gave added impetus. And the desire to highlight real and potential threats as we approach the 21st century, along with their possible solutions, turned an inspiration into a feeling of compulsion.

Jeremy Early, March 1997

CHAPTER 1

Shaping the Present

Cynics tend to subscribe to the view that progress means deterioration. Environmentally they may well have a point, and they would certainly have had a point if plans put forward for the River Mole two or three hundred years ago had come to fruition. Instead of the narrow channels and mild meanders we see today, there might have been at best sufficient width and depth for vessels of up to 20 tons, and at worst a massive, probably now decayed, canal. The former was the proposal of Andrew Yarranton, who surveyed the river in the 1690s and reported it fit to be made navigable to transport "good and vast quantities of timber to build ships…coals, corn and all other commodities…to and from London." This was 30 years or so after an Act was passed by Parliament, but never executed, granting permission for the Mole to be made navigable from below Reigate to the River Thames.

Nothing came of Yarranton's plan, or of a proposal in 1811 for a canal to be built between Holmwood and Thames Ditton via Leatherhead. Then in 1825 Nicholas Wilcox Cundy sprang up with the greatest plan of all – the Grand Imperial Ship Canal. As the History of Leatherhead, edited by Edwina Vardey, reveals: "[Cundy] planned a canal 150 ft wide and 28 ft deep able to accommodate the largest ships afloat. It was to run 78 miles from Rotherhithe to Spithead passing through Wandsworth, Malden, Epsom Common to Leatherhead Bridge and on to Mickleham, Dorking and Arundel." Canals are not bad for wildlife *per se* – in Surrey the Basingstoke Canal, and to a lesser extent the Wey Navigation, prove as much – but it is hard to believe alterations on the scale advocated by Cundy would have been beneficial in the short or the long term. Fortunately nothing came of his scheme, due principally to the projected cost, but this is not to say man has had no influence on the river.

THE MOLE – HUMAN IMPACTS

In all societies the environment, even where it seems wildest and freest, reflects the people who have lived in it. What we see, and perhaps more importantly what we do not see, are a direct consequence of human actions and decisions. Fresh, flowing water has been an invaluable resource since time immemorial but overflowing water is not always so useful, despite the improvement in soil productivity to which it can lead. For all the many attempts to control it, the Mole still has a natural floodplain which 'goes under' to a depth of up to a foot in parts most winters. These short-lived mini-floods reveal the natural character of the river and hint at its power, but they do not compare with the monumental burstings of banks which occurred in 1852, 1890 and September 1968. The last-named will be remembered by many local residents, and on the subject of the October 1852 version, diarist Miss Amelia Hunter wrote: "River still swollen. The inhabitants of the cottages at Leatherhead Bridge obliged to occupy their upper rooms. Ducks floating in at their doors."

In Roman times the whole of the river valley would have consisted of fen and marsh. While drainage for agriculture probably started in the late-Saxon period, large swathes of land would still have been inundated for a fair part of each year. The flood water had a beneficial effect by adding nutrients, neutralising any soil acidity and promoting the growth of grasses, and it enabled top-quality grazing by cattle in the months after the hay had been cut. As in virtually every other part of the country, notably the Fens, relentless and skilled drainage schemes eventually eliminated the valley marsh and wet meadows, though some survived for a considerable time. In his seminal essay on the River Mole in the Proceedings of the Leatherhead and District Local History Society for 1964, A T Ruby provided this fascinating footnote to the drainage question: "A number of newcomers to the locality may have no idea that 25 years ago the ground on which they dwell was covered with rushes and marsh vegetation."

With the farming which it facilitated, drainage has probably had the most dramatic consequences of all for the river and its immediate vicinity. However, industrial and commercial activity, and urban development, have also left their mark around Leatherhead. There were mills at Thorncroft, Leatherhead Bridge (a tannery) and Fetcham Splash – a map showing all the locations mentioned in the text is on page 17. There is the business park virtually on the riverbank north-west of the town centre. There is the railway line to Guildford, which led to the river being artificially straightened for 150 metres near Fetcham. And there are numerous concrete/steel outflows carrying run-off of various kinds into the river from a wide area. From the 1950s to the 1970s the Common Meadow bordering the river was used as playing fields by employees of Ronsons' cigarette lighter factory.

On top of this there are seven bridges, including four within 400 metres of each other west of Leatherhead town, together with a number of large houses and less grandiose dwellings fronting the river between Thorncroft Bridge and Waterway Road. The effect of these houses has not been merely a physical presence of bricks and mortar, for the wealthier property owners exerted a significant influence on the river. Trees were planted on the banks and islands, which were used for relaxation, and boathouses and weirs were constructed to help ensure a suitable depth of water for boating. The southern channel downstream from Thorncroft Bridge was cut as a canal around 1770 for the owner of Thorncroft Manor, and the renowned landscape gardener Capability Brown is presumed to have designed the nearby Shell Bridge.

The fact that at a water carnival in July 1901 the town band played on the main island near Leatherhead Bridge while encircled by a procession of illuminated boats indicates the extent to which that island was clear of trees and undergrowth – clearer than now, anyway. On the whole, though, the uses mentioned in the preceding paragraph did not place undue pressure on the habitat. They almost certainly had less effect on the flora and fauna than subsequent developments, principally a dramatic growth in population over the last 70 years, and everything this has entailed in the way of a burgeoning infrastructure, accompanied by increased pollution, sewage and waste.

Due to lack of detailed information it is impossible to be precise about what wildlife there was a century or more ago, and some of the limited evidence we have is conflicting. In his History of Leatherhead published in 1821, the vicar James Dallaway mentioned only five "notable" species of bird in his garden by the river – nightingale, blackcap, moorhen, kingfisher and wren. With the exception of the nightingale, which now has its nearest location at Bookham Common, these species are still around, but others that nested locally, even into this century, are not. They include corncrake, snipe, red-backed shrike, wryneck and yellow wagtail.

We have precious few reliable records of invertebrates but it is probable that numbers and varieties of butterflies, and of dragonflies and damselflies, to name the two most obvious groups, have declined. Mammals have not done well either – there are no brown hares now, and no otters. The latter were reportedly present on the Mole near Leatherhead in 1909, and in 1945 R S R Fitter wrote in his book London's Natural History: "[Otters] frequent the rivers Lea, Stort, Mole, and probably also the Colne." Against this, Dallaway had observed in 1821 that the species was quite rare, "two only having been taken opposite my garden in the course of the last 30 years." Although there are hopes of a comeback by the otter along the River Wey, it will require a miracle for this lovely creature to regain a foothold on the Mole. Rounding things off, the local brown trout used to be famous across Europe, but while they can still be seen now and then – there are more up towards Cobham – it would take another miracle, or systematic stocking, for any angler to catch the species on a regular basis at Leatherhead.

Add to all these disappearances an unspecified loss of flora, and it is obvious that a great deal has gone. Leatherhead is far from unique in this respect – otters, corncrakes, red-backed shrikes and snipe, to name just four, have disappeared from many of their former haunts in Britain. The change has not been for the better anywhere, but concentrating on the local 'patch' once again, maybe one should be careful about lauding the good old days too vigorously. In 1914, in A Pilgrimage in Surrey, James Ogilvy wrote that Leatherhead Bridge used to offer "one of the most cheerful stretches of the Mole, [running] briskly over a clear, pebbly bed." Starkly, he continued: "Now it is the old story – crude tar dressings on the roads carried by the surface drains into the river and every living thing vanished from the waters." An idyllic spot had become "merely a melancholy drain [with] a tangled growth of sedges and water weeds."

THE MOLE – WATER QUALITY

For all Ogilvy's gloom, the Mole runs briskly over a clear, pebbly bed at Leatherhead Bridge today. Yet his words do have resonance in the 1990s on account of the situation with run-off. Unlike foul sewers, surface water drains and sewers are designed to carry rainwater directly to water courses untreated, because the liquid is deemed harmless. Despite this view, oil, diesel, petrol, antifreeze, and various metals, can all be deposited by vehicles, while salted grit is deposited for them. After abundant rain, much of whatever is lying on local roads, and on some of the numerous car parks, enters the river. In addition, waste oil, including that from householders with cars, plus detergent used to wash vehicles, are not always disposed of as they should be through the foul sewer.

Although the higher levels of water that occur after rain encourage the process of dilution, none of the attacks just mentioned help in the battle for water purity. In the last 20 years regular surveys have been carried out at River Lane, Fetcham, and at a number of other sites along the 80-kilometre length of the Mole and its numerous tributaries. Initially these were done by the Nature Conservancy Council and Thames Water Authority but when the Water Act was passed in 1989, the then newly-founded National Rivers Authority (NRA) became the responsible body. The samples, along with two fisheries surveys since 1986, give a clear picture of the health of the water, largely because of the careful scientific analysis of macroinvertebrates which is involved. These creatures include shrimps, worms and the larvae of such insects as mayflies and caddis flies. They are excellent indicators of the environmental quality of a river because they are unable to move very far and they respond to everything contained in the water, such as pollutants which occur only infrequently or at very low levels.

While there is still plenty of room for improvement, the river is cleaner chemically than it was 20 or even 10 years ago. The surveys scientifically demonstrate as much, so this is a matter of data, not opinion. To give one of the most important sources of evidence, dragonfly and damselfly nymphs are acknowledged to be among the best possible indicators of clean conditions. The majority live in the water for around two years and are highly susceptible to pollution. At River Lane none were present in the samples taken before 1986 but since that date they have been found consistently and seem to be increasing. The white-legged damselfly, one of the least tolerant of all to pollution, is back breeding in a number of places. Using the NRA's General Quality Assessment scheme, which takes into account chemistry, nutrients, aesthetics and biology, from 1992-1994 the whole of the section of the Mole under consideration in this book was rated Grade B on a scale that runs from A (best) to F.

Improvements in water quality were beginning to occur before 1989 but there is no doubt that the NRA has been of considerable importance in continuing and accelerating the process. The organisation has relentlessly monitored the water, has educated business interests, the farming community and the public regarding the prevention of pollution, and has energetically pursued and prosecuted polluters. With a maximum fine of £20,000 available to magistrates under the Water Resources Act 1991, no commercial concern can afford to treat the water environment with impunity.

On 1st April 1996 the NRA was amalgamated with Her Majesty's Inspectorate of Pollution and the waste regulation authorities under the umbrella of the Environment Agency. Fortunately this has had no damaging effect on the NRA's sterling work, an issue of paramount importance. Officially, agricultural and industrial pollution on the Mole is low, but the figures for 1990-95 still show a total of 828 reported pollution incidents, which the NRA broke down into one major, 47 significant and 780 minor. There is no such thing as beneficial pollution. Acute incidents receive the lion's share of publicity but minor and unreported ones have a cumulative force which, while not so devastating as a major oil spillage, is not to be

underestimated, especially as it is insidious. One significant incident in July 1995 involved 20,000 litres of detergent entering the river south of Reigate, killing hundreds of fish. Prompt action by the emergency services prevented further damage, but what happened there confirmed the extent to which the Mole's wildlife lives on a knife-edge.

Superficially, some comfort may be gleaned from the fact that the Leatherhead stretch is reasonably well removed from all the discharges which assault the river in the upper reaches due to the influence of Crawley, the A23/M23 corridor and Gatwick Airport. The 48 major or significant pollution incidents just noted, in which oil and chemicals together outscored any of their rivals, included four near Leatherhead, three near Dorking – and over 30 in the Horley-Crawley area. Yet local complacency on that score is completely out of place because the Mole is not a succession of isolated sections of water. It is an organic whole.

THE MOLE – HABITAT AND WILDLIFE

Despite the losses, despite the problems, despite worries about the future which will come under the spotlight in Chapter 6, nature enthusiasts are not faced with a wildlife void in the Mole corridor at Leatherhead.

There have been arrivals in the last half-century or so, including mandarin duck and migrant hawker dragonfly, both a positive influence, and mink, a negative influence. My personal observation over nearly 10 years has revealed getting on for 100 species of bird, around 20 species of both mammals and butterflies, and 15 species of dragonfly; a checklist is on pages 92-93. Five small-scale annual breeding species of bird are on the new `Red List' of 36 species in crisis contained in the 1996 Birds of Conservation Concern Report produced by eight leading conservation organisations. They are bullfinch, reed bunting, skylark, song thrush and spotted flycatcher. The river between Young Street and the Common Meadow is designated as a Site of Nature Conservation Importance in the Mole Valley Local Plan. Moreover, the Mole, while not of such consistently high ecological quality to enable it to be made a Site of Special Scientific Interest under the Wildlife and Countryside Act 1981, has a high grading using the criteria applied by the London Ecology Unit. In a river corridor survey carried out for the NRA in 1992 by the Environmental Consultancy of the University of Sheffield, the section from Leatherhead Bridge to Fetcham Splash was rated Grade 1, or officially "critically important for wildlife [and] a possible candidate for protective status". This was due to the "rich and varied aquatic flora", abundant and varied dragonflies and the scarce nature of the habitat. The stretch from Young Street to Leatherhead Bridge was rated Grade 2, or officially "important for wildlife".

To put a little flesh on these bones, the habitat, and the best sites for seeing some of the more notable species, are as follows. Geologically there is considerable variety for such a limited area, with alluvium and gravel along the river, bordered successively from south to north by chalk, Thanet sand, Reading/Woolwich beds and London clay. The soil for the most part is shallow, well-drained and loamy while the underlying water-rich chalk aquifer feeds the river through springs both south (at Thorncroft) and north of Leatherhead. Public access to the river is better than almost anywhere else in the catchment, via footpaths close to the west bank from Young Street to Leatherhead Bridge and close to the east bank from the bridge to the end of the Common Meadow. There is also a 100-metre stretch of made-up path on the east bank leading to Leatherhead Bridge, along Minchin Close. At Fetcham Splash full access exists near the crossing.

Between Young Street – the best local site for kestrels – and Thorncroft Bridge the river runs north north-east and consists of a narrow, winding channel about 12 metres wide with quite steep, partly-wooded banks. From Thorncroft Bridge the river runs north-west. In the section up to Leatherhead Bridge there are two main channels and a couple of shallow subsidiary ones, around a group of four islands which are well-wooded with a mixture of trees dominated by alder and ash. Birds to be seen near Thorncroft include treecreepers and both great and lesser spotted woodpeckers, especially during March-April before the trees come into leaf. A water vole was noted here in 1990, but sadly this species is suffering a grave national decline, and searches of the middle Mole during 1996 revealed no sign of them. The banking is quite deep along the northern channel, where kingfishers nest annually, but much shallower on the south. The fields near the Leisure Centre and Leatherhead FC ground are good for green woodpeckers, and in winter the nearby hawthorn bushes are reliable for redwing. This area also offers a decent opportunity to see song thrushes.

At Leatherhead Bridge the river reverts to one channel, staying that way until dividing again briefly at Fetcham Splash. This bridge, where the Mole has its widest point, nearly 70 metres across, is a hot spot for grey wagtails, bats and, on occasions, mink. Native crayfish are also believed to breed close by. This vulnerable species is one of 116 listed in the conservation proposals made by the Government-sponsored Biodiversity Steering Group at the end of 1995. Public seats by a small pond at Mansion Garden on the north-east bank afford an excellent – and comfortable – chance to view grey herons, mandarin ducks, little grebes and kingfishers, though the odds against seeing them all at one sitting are pretty long. Kingfishers can be glimpsed virtually anywhere along the river, and at virtually any time of day and year, but the best month is probably July, when the adults are feverishly seeking food for their nestlings.

There are buildings on both banks near the bridge, but after Waterway Road – along Riverside Walk – more natural cover for wildlife appears, with a small and fairly dense copse on the embankment between the two railway bridges. Sparrowhawks, jays and blackcaps nest annually, and holly blue butterflies can be very evident. In summer, bush crickets are common on undergrowth before the Guildford line railway bridge, and moles can be highly active – over 70 hills appeared in a couple of months along a 25-metre stretch during the winter of 1995-96. On the far bank between the railway bridges is a mixture of open meadow, scrub, hedge and secondary woodland, some of which unfortunately was cleared during 1996. This is a consistent area for roe deer, foxes and bullfinches; stoats and a weasel have been sighted. Not to be outdone, the river between the railway bridges, all 120 metres of it, provided a memorable half-hour's bird watching on a snowy New Year's Day in 1997, with a perched kingfisher, a heron, a gadwall, a common snipe, a pair of goosanders, four tufted ducks and four little grebes.

From the Guildford line railway bridge to the Common Meadow little cover exists, due to River Cottage on the south-west bank and the business park to the north-east. The few trees are predominantly alder and the plants include brambles, nettles (some with parasitic greater dodder, a nationally scarce species) and Himalayan balsam. This is the best section of the river for damselflies, notably the banded demoiselle, the large red and the white-legged, and for dragonflies, notably Britain's biggest, the emperor. Among the species of butterfly present – albeit not in great quantities – are orange tip, large skipper, small skipper, green-veined white, peacock and comma. Moths include angle shades and white ermine. In the bank-side vegetation are various beetles, such as the cardinal; crab, orb-web and wolf spiders; scorpion flies and adult caddis flies; and brightly-coloured snails. Birds are headed by nesting long-tailed tits, by goldfinches and by wintering siskins and, less often, redpolls. The banks are of reasonable depth, as is the river, with pike not uncommon.

The flat, open Common Meadow was registered as a common by the Leatherhead & District Countryside Protection Society in 1968. There is minimal cover on the north-east bank of the river, and initially only crack willow trees on the other side, where an arable field separates those trees from the railway embankment. Both banks are fairly shallow, as is the water, with shoals of minnows common. Birds seen year-round on the river are little grebes and moorhens, with the latter numerous. Cormorants visit irregularly, and wintering species are headed by tufted ducks and

goosanders, both mentioned already. The last-named have been turning up consistently in recent years, chiefly towards the end of the Meadow – there was a maximum count of 15 in January 1996. Spring/autumn migrants include common and, more rarely, green sandpipers. Meadow pipits are annual autumn visitors on the Common Meadow, where lapwing drop by in the spring and green woodpeckers, mistle thrushes and pied wagtails are a feature in all seasons.

At the end of the meadow, south of Randalls Park Crematorium, there is a mixed deciduous wood and a section of scrub containing hawthorn trees, dog rose and spindle. This is a reliable site for roe deer, badgers, rabbits and, in winter, redwing and fieldfare. A line of hawthorn and bramble, interspersed with oak, ash and plane, borders the scrub and separates it from the Meadow at a distance of about 100 metres from the river. Here little owls can be seen on occasions, bullfinches and spotted flycatchers have bred through the 1990s, and yellowhammers nested until 1991.

En route to Fetcham Splash the river turns due west, with a small island and some quite deep banking on the southern flank, where kingfishers sometimes breed, followed by open grassland. To the north, apart from where the Crematorium lawn goes right down to the water, cover is excellent, with mixed woodland including oak, yew, beech and frequent holly and laurel. In winter tufted ducks are regular on the river, and six teal were seen in January 1997. Little owls and woodpeckers have nested in the wood, and tawny owls are heard now and then. The Splash – quite good for grey wagtails – has a wide (20 metres) and a narrow channel, with plentiful emergent vegetation, suitable for dragonflies.

FETCHAM MILL POND – DECLINE AND RENEWAL

The Mole has suffered much more than it deserves at the hands of humans. In some respects the same can be said of Fetcham Mill Pond, which lies only 70 metres or so from the river and is one of Mole Valley's least appreciated, but most precious, jewels.

The 1990s version would be unrecognisable to anyone who knew the spot around the turn of the century. In those days the mill, which had existed in one shape or another from at least the 13th century, was still functioning – it ceased when burned down in 1917 – and the Pond had altered little in shape or character for many decades. In Highways and Byways in Surrey, published in 1908, Eric Parker enthused that the Pond "slopes gradually from the sides over a chalky bottom, and is of an intense clear green. Here and there are open spaces in the weeds; patches of deeper blue-green, which can be seen, if you look closely, to be moving – a most uncanny motion. The water wells up incredibly fast and quiet, and surely incredibly cold, from some unplumbed, invisible source below. No frost ever sets ice on the millpond, it is said, and in hard winters wildfowl flock to it. There is a strong spell of magic over all that strange pool. Some naiad Circe combs her hair far below the weeds and has bewitched the wildfowl and the green cold water."

Naiad or no, the Mill Pond, which is exceptional in lying above the fields immediately surrounding it, was fed by 11 springs bubbling up funnels of lime deposits rising through a bed of gravel to chalk. The reliability of this water supply was one factor which encouraged the owners, Messrs Mizen Bros., to plant over three hectares of watercress beds in the 1920s. In 1931 they also reclaimed much of the Pond at the Cobham Road end by dumping surplus material. Cress requires huge amounts of irrigation. What with these requirements, those of market garden produce in five hectares of glasshouses, fresh demands by the Water Undertaking, and the construction of the pumping station in Waterway Road, the Pond all but dried up.

Indeed, it did dry up in the 'drought summer' of 1947, and a few years later in his book Old Surrey Water-Mills, J Hillier wrote: "The pond is a sorry sight – practically dry, save for one deep part where the water remains and where the swans, looking far too large for so negligible a puddle, appear uncomfortable." He continued: "The uneven bottom of the pool – grey, parched and cracked, with a litter of unsightly rubbish the water used mercifully to cover – is an ugly sight." Without a shred of hope, Hillier concluded: "The scene hereabouts has changed so much in the last 20 years, the country has been so far won over to suburbia, that the retention of a small stretch of water, when the meadows that surrounded it are streets of houses, would be an anachronism."

Luckily rescue was at hand, because when Mizen Bros. ceased trading in 1957, East Surrey Water Co. (ESW) took over the Pond and much of the land around it, while another part went to the bus company, which constructed a depot there. The water company capped the springs, reducing the size of the Pond still further, lined it with waterproof sheeting and impervious silt, and used a borehole to keep the water at a generally consistent level – the maximum depth is just over a metre. A pumping station was built and the company gained authorisation to abstract a maximum of three million gallons a day from the aquifer. The end result of all this activity – Leatherhead's new fire station was opened just to the south in 1969 – was a reduction in the size of the Pond from something in the region of 400 metres long by 80 metres wide, to 300 metres long by 70 metres wide.

The physical changes and changes of use at the Mill Pond not only cut its size; predictably, they also reduced the species to be found. As with the river, one cannot be specific about the 19th century, though it is worth noting that the site was well-known then for nightingales. The recent past is a different matter, and Jeffery Wheatley of the Surrey Bird Club reveals that at various stages in the period 1959-1961 there were maxima of 16 teal, 12 water rail, 75 moorhens, 200 rooks and 120 lapwing, while in the early 1930s a dozen pairs of little grebe bred there, with autumn flocks of around 50. Those are figures present-day watchers can only dream about, yet there are still some splendid species, as the following section shows.

FETCHAM MILL POND – HABITAT AND WILDLIFE

Access at the Mill Pond is restricted to a public footpath which runs between Mill Lane and

Cobham Road on the northern bank, and goes right by the water for about 100 metres. There are also partial views from the pavement along Cobham Road. The water is both clear and pure and half the surface area is fringed by a shallow mixture of emergent vegetation including reed mace and sedges, with several crack willow trees on the southern side. A small wooded island towards the northern bank has sallow, sycamore and ash with dense bramble thickets and nettles. Mute swans and mallards nest on the island, and greenfinches, willow warblers, chiffchaffs and long-tailed tits in the trees and bushes. Other breeding waterbirds are little grebes, moorhens and coots. A black redstart was reportedly on the premises in spring 1996, and summer visitors are spearheaded by swifts and house martins, which stay around for longer than the annual sand martins. Kingfishers drop in regularly and common terns sometimes spend a day or two fishing in the autumn on their way south to Africa. The most abundant wintering species is the black-headed gull, with up to 200. More notable, though less apparent, are water rail, gadwall, tufted duck, pochard, teal and occasionally shoveler and goosander. A smew spent a short time here in January 1997.

The Pond is superb for damselflies and dragonflies, with the azure damselfly, common blue damselfly, blue-tailed damselfly, black-tailed skimmer and common darter among the most obvious of 11 breeding species. In all probability one reason behind the increase in dragonfly numbers along the river, especially at Riverside Walk, has been the presence of the Mill Pond close by acting as a reliable nursery, or force for

colonisation, once the water quality in the Mole improved. Rudd are the commonest fish, with pike often also visible. Grass snakes are sighted now and then, and common frogs and toads used to spawn in large numbers but have declined.

Flat, coarsely mown, improved grassland to the south of the Pond, where the common blue butterfly maintains a precarious foothold and grasshoppers can be numerous in summer, is crossed by a marshy, reed-filled duct running from the pumping station towards the fire station and eventually going into the Mole. About 50 metres from Cobham Road, this plays host annually to breeding sedge warblers and reed buntings, though only in small numbers; reed warblers have also bred. In the winter up to 40 common snipe and one or two jack snipe can be found in the duct. To the east of the Pond are Mill Cottage, a line of conifers bordering Mill Lane containing breeding goldcrest, and a shed with a miniature railway track used by the Surrey Society of Model Engineers. To the north-west lies an arable field where skylarks and lapwing have bred lately. A flock of 65 lapwing was present early in 1996, and respectable numbers of linnet turn up some years in winter. Brown rats can be numerous. On the edge of the field nearest the railway embankment lies a seasonally marshy area.

For the record, the Mill Pond was surveyed as a potential Site of Nature Conservation Importance in the early 1990s, but as the flora and fauna were not considered significant on a county basis, despite being important locally, it was not included in the final list of 102 sites in the Mole Valley Local Plan.

In 1964, A T Ruby wrote: "So far as is known, there is nothing peculiar or striking among the natural denizens of the river and its immediate vicinity." The species listed in this chapter give the lie to that comment. They also provide excellent opportunities for nature watchers, all within a fairly short walk of Leatherhead town centre, in an area closely bordered by two communities with a combined population of 18,000. Granted, in a casual stroll of half an hour one is unlikely to see vast quantities of wildlife even in the most prolific months, May and June. But a good few should appear in a watchful 30 minutes, and while cursory attention can be rewarding, patience and persistence guarantee a tenfold return. The photographs which appear in the next four chapters aim to prove the point by revealing the habitat and just some of the life it holds through the seasons. A number of the species illustrated are conspicuous, a number are invariably hidden, but all are jewels deserving to be cherished.

The River Mole at Leatherhead

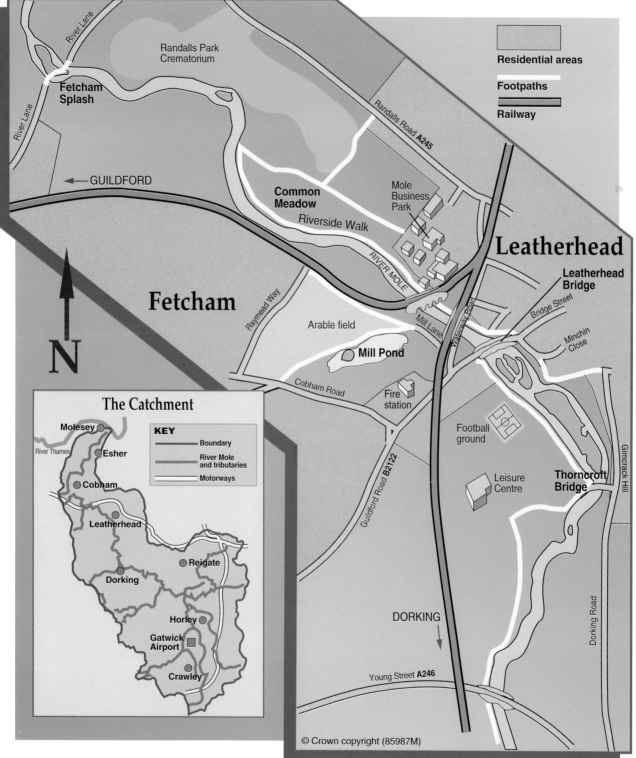

Residential areas

Footpaths

Railway

River Lane

Randalls Park
Crematorium

Fetcham
Splash

River Lane

← GUILDFORD

Randalls Road **A245**

Common
Meadow

Riverside Walk

Mole
Business
Park

RIVER MOLE

Leatherhead

**Leatherhead
Bridge**

Bridge Street

Minchin
Close

Fetcham

Raymead Way

Arable field

Mill Lane

Walsway Road

N

Mill Pond

Cobham Road

Fire
station

Football
ground

Gimcrack Hill

The Catchment

Molesey

River Thames

Esher

Cobham

KEY

Boundary

River Mole
and tributaries

Motorways

Leatherhead

Reigate

Dorking

Guildford Road **B2122**

Leisure
Centre

**Thorncroft
Bridge**

Dorking Road

Horley

Gatwick
Airport

Crawley

DORKING
↓

Young Street **A246**

© Crown copyright (85987M)

Black-tailed skimmer *dragonfly*
basking near Fetcham Mill Pond

CHAPTER 2

For winter's rains and ruins are over,
And all the season of snows and sins;
The days dividing lover and lover,
The light that loses, the night that wins;
And time remembered is grief forgotten,
And frosts are slain and flowers begotten,
And in green underwood and cover
Blossom by blossom the spring begins.

ALGERNON SWINBURNE, Spring

*Also known as ramsons, **wood garlic** thrives in damp areas along the river-bank, creating dense stands where the garlic smell is pronounced*

*A highly territorial resident of woodland and sunny margins, the **speckled wood** lives in a world of dappled light perfectly suited to its colouring. There are at least two broods each year, with sightings for much of the period from mid-April to mid-September*

The largest and arguably most characteristic bird of Leatherhead's waterways, with a wingspan of two metres, the **mute swan** mates in March-April. Once the act is completed, the cob and pen rise up and virtually dance on the water

Coots (below) often seem to exist mainly to engage in noisy arguments but there is no doubting the loyalty of a breeding pair, nor their resolution in protecting their offspring. Up to five pairs breed on the Mill Pond each year, starting in March

The **kingfisher** *is protected under British and EU law and is the jewel in the crown of the River Mole, breeding every year in respectable numbers, with a couple of broods if all goes well. Just 17cm in length, including a 40mm bill, the kingfisher eats some invertebrates but feeds mainly on small fish, caught by diving into the water. A breeding pair with four young need the best part of 100 fish a day. Fortunately the Mole is well-stocked with the main prey,* **minnows** *(left) and miller's thumb*

***Red campion** does well by the Mole from May to September. The flowers are scentless and individual plants can grow to a height of a metre*

*The **moorhen** (below) is a fairly shy bird of great mobility, equally at home in still and flowing water. There are usually two broods each year and although losses can be high, the species is gaining in strength, especially along the river*

Swans *can build their sizeable nests from any suitable vegetation, including reeds, grasses and twigs, but the pictured nest consists of straw provided by an RSPCA inspector. The pen lays up to 11 eggs – the average is six – and incubation lasts five weeks. Nests are vulnerable to flooding, particularly on the Mole, and the forlorn consequence of heavy rain in 1990 is shown on the left. Most broods hatch in May*

*The Common Meadow is usually a sea of yellow in June thanks to copious **meadow buttercups***

*The web of an **orb-web spider** (below) glistens with dew after a cool, misty night in spring. Once the sun gets going the dew disappears and the web, constructed of liquid protein by the female, becomes invisible, regaining its customary lethal efficiency*

*There is no shortage of **red foxes**, which are essentially nocturnal and have the best of both worlds, able to forage in urban and rural surroundings where they eat anything from hedgehogs to windfall apples. Vixens have litters of up to five cubs in underground dens in March-April. Boisterous play-fighting (right) is part of the learning process, teaching skills vital in adulthood*

*This dozing **grey heron** is concealing all of its lengthy neck, which when extended takes the bird's height to a metre. While easy to observe along the Mole and at the Mill Pond, herons do not breed here due to a lack of appropriate woodland*

Once **cygnets** leave the nest they can fall prey to cold or predators, including heron and pike. As a safeguard, the pen often carries the youngsters on her back for the first week or so (right). Swans are highly protective parents – the two above are 'fluffed up' because another adult has just flown over

The Mill Pond is at its most beguiling in June, with colourful sedges and reeds, crack willows in full leaf, and abundant cover on the island, all of which help the varied birdlife

Water-crowfoot, *from the buttercup family, is suited by shallow water. The variable flow of the Mole through rainfall results in inconsistent flowering, with the best site downstream of Leatherhead Bridge*

Mallards *(below) are the commonest local water bird, with a count of 85 on the Mill Pond in September 1995. Ducklings are visible every month from April to July or even August, with large broods, sometimes into double figures. Wastage, though, is considerable due to the elements and other animals*

*Not all species of **mayfly** hatch in May, but the largest, with a 25mm body, does. They are impossible to miss swarming in the evening around the river, especially on warm days. The water-based nymphs live for two years but the flying adults for just one day*

*Though only 10mm long, the **crab spider** (below) is a mobile and deadly predator, which lies in wait on foliage for passing insects. The long front legs are particularly powerful*

*Our largest damselfly, with a wingspan of 60mm and a length of 45mm, the **banded demoiselle** is prolific along the Mole from May to August. This is a female; the male has a blue body and blue patches on the wings which, as with nearly all damselflies, are held parallel to the body at rest*

*In its element in shallow, fast-flowing water, the **grey wagtail** preys on insects, including damselflies, and finds ideal conditions near the town. Happy to take advantage of man-made structures, they regularly nest in holes in the railway bridges crossing the river*

Nettles provide sustenance for several common species of butterfly, including comma, peacock and, below, **small tortoiseshell**, whose females can lay up to 200 eggs in one cluster. The caterpillars (left) consume huge quantities of nettles in growing to 22mm in a month but only a fraction survive to pupate. Adults, with a wingspan of around 55mm, often bask. They come in two broods and can be seen most months – the second brood hibernates

*Tipping the scales at only 10 grams, the **sedge warbler** winters in Africa before trekking north to breed, arriving in late-April. Males sing relentlessly, mixing sweet and sour notes in a vigorous chatter aimed at attracting a mate. Suited by waterside vegetation, these dynamos are not numerous near Leatherhead and head south in September*

CHAPTER 3

Summer

The English summer is pleasanter than that of any other country in Europe, on no other account but because it has a greater mixture of spring in it. The mildness of our climate, with those frequent refreshments of dews and rains that fall among us, keep up a perpetual cheerfulness in our fields, and fill the hottest months of the year with a lively verdure.

JOSEPH ADDISON, The Spectator

A damp-loving species of the river-bank, **purple loosestrife** is a striking feature from July to September, but one which is being swamped in places by invasive Himalayan balsam

The **common blue** butterfly (below) has two generations each year and, though rare in the area, with luck it can be glimpsed between June and September. The butterfly – wingspan 35mm – is very active in sunshine and frequently visits flowers including bird's-foot trefoil, the food-plant of the caterpillars

The reappearance of the **white-legged damselfly** along the Mole is a testimony to improvements in water quality. It is one of the most attractive of all damselflies, and one of the largest at 35mm in length. This is a male – the female is green – and they are on the wing in June and July

Fox cub mortality is high, but by August the survivors are able to forage for themselves even though the family remains a unit. The cubs are not fully grown until September, and the family group starts to break up in October

The **gatekeeper** (below), or hedge brown, is a plentiful high-summer species near sunny hedgerows and in rough, grassy, scrubby locations such as the Common Meadow. The large compound eyes provide excellent vision, and the long antennae are essential sensory organs

Dragonfly nymphs live in the water for up to two years and are formidable predators. Metamorphosis into the full flying adult occurs on vegetation early in the day, as with this **common darter** at the Mill Pond. The seemingly cramped larval case the insect has just left is close by, and the 'anaemic' look is typical of a drying-out hatchling

Greater dodder *is a rootless, twining parasite lacking chlorophyll which smothers its host, usually the stinging nettle. A nationally scarce species, it is very obvious from July to September near the business park along Riverside Walk*

Every **swan** *(below) is fastidious about its plumage, preening and bathing vigorously. An adult has more than 25,000 feathers and can weigh up to 14kg, so there is quite a splash at bath time*

*The Mill Pond at 6am in July. The
stillness found early on some summer
mornings ensures excellent reflections*

Roe deer – *buck right, doe and the buck's three-month-old fawn below – are present in significant numbers. Athletic and small, only 66cm at the shoulder, they can turn up almost anywhere but are not always easy to spot. This is due first to their crepuscular habits and secondly to their caution combined with acute sense of hearing and smell*

*Though similarly carnivorous, damselflies are smaller than dragonflies, with a feebler, more fluttery flight and a greater tendency to settle. The **common blue damselfly** is strongly represented at the Mill Pond and along the river from June to the end of August. This pair is mating in what is known as the 'copulation wheel', after which eggs are laid on aquatic vegetation*

From the same order as grasshoppers, but 'fatter' and with much longer antennae, the 25mm **dark bush cricket** is seen, though more often heard, mainly on brambles from August to October. The female's scimitar-like ovipositor is used to deposit eggs in the ground

The **large skipper** butterfly has a wingspan of up to 35mm and is visible from mid-June to the end of July at the Mill Pond and along Riverside Walk. Moth-like in appearance, they fly principally in sunshine and settle frequently

The **garden spider** will feed on just about anything falling foul of its web, including here a common field grasshopper. The spider bites the victim, causing paralysis, then wraps it and injects enzymes to reduce the body tissues to liquid for consumption

Coots (below) make assiduous parents to broods of up to six, fulfilling their duties for longer than many birds. In winter their numbers are boosted by migrants from the north and east

*Like the red admiral, the **painted lady** (opposite) is an annual migrant of above-average size, measuring 65mm. A few usually turn up locally during May-June and August-September, the spring brood having flown from North Africa. Their breeding leads to the second, home-bred batch, which is incapable of surviving the British winter*

*Despite its size, the **grey heron** is not heavy, weighing in at under 2kg. The varied diet – fish, amphibians, small mammals, birds – is obtained in or close to shallow water. Prey is invariably taken after patient waiting rather than through energetic tactics*

51

A July species, sighted irregularly, the **ringlet** is 50mm across. Active even in cloudy weather, it is suited by damp habitats with a thick growth of the native grasses on which the caterpillars feed

Sunset over the Mole at the Common Meadow

Some alien species are unwelcome but the **mandarin duck** (above) poses no threat to native wildlife and as a bonus looks superb, especially the dazzling male. Although endangered in parts of their Asian homelands, these tree nesters are doing splendidly in Surrey, with around 800 pairs, and the Mole is a stronghold

Brought to Britain from the Balkans in the 17th century, the **horse chestnut** is evident by the river between Young Street and Thorncroft Bridge. Its leaves are among the first to arrive in spring, and the first to 'turn' in autumn

The **migrant hawker** dragonfly is the smallest of the hawker group and is a major success story, having progressively colonised much of southern Britain in the last 50 years. This pair is mating on greater reed mace at the Mill Pond, with the blue-black male on top and the yellow-brown female below. The species can be seen readily from August to October

CHAPTER 4
Autumn

There is a beautiful spirit breathing now,
Its mellow richness on the clustered trees,
And, from a beaker full of richest dyes,
Pouring new glory on the autumn woods,
And dipping in warm light the pillared clouds.

HENRY LONGFELLOW, Autumn

Kingfishers *are naturally territorial and even juveniles show aggressive tendencies, always assuming they can find a stretch of water unoccupied by adults. The bird above, full of tension and showing its beak in threatening posture, is a female aged around two months. Opposite, the pair displaying against each other in typically upright fashion are a similar age, and could even be siblings*

The fruits, or **hips**, of wild roses are an important food source for birds

The **peacock** (below) is one of our largest butterflies, with a wingspan of almost 70mm, and one of the handsomest. Powerful fliers who nectar on various flowers, often in gardens, they have one brood, emerging in August and overwintering

*The **common darter** is the smallest resident dragonfly, with a wingspan of 60mm, and the easiest to approach. After a cool autumn night this female is covered in dew and will be unable to fly until warming up. In sunny years, the species continues through to October*

Present in rough, open places, including the Common Meadow, the **small copper** (opposite) has a wingspan of around 30mm and produces three broods, in May, July-August and, given a good summer, September. The food-plant is sorrel

Unlike a number of the maple breed, **field maple** is a native species. They rarely grow tall but consistently provide a stunning show in autumn

Providing **cygnets** (below) get past the first fortnight of life they stand a fair chance of surviving in the medium term. The family stays together until at least October, and sometimes into the new year

By October, as food runs out, that voracious aphid-eater the **seven-spot ladybird** *(above) is starting to look for a place to hibernate. The striking colour acts as a warning to predators, indicating the presence of alkaloid poisons*

*Berries, including **holly** and hawthorn, provide vital nourishment for such birds as redwing and fieldfare*

With a wingspan of 100mm and a length of 75mm, the **brown hawker** is second only to the emperor in size among dragonflies and is widespread from July to October, patrolling from dawn to dusk at speeds of up to 30mph. This female is a recent hatchling. Note the enormous compound eyes, which have 30,000 facets and provide all-round vision

*Once frost arrives in late autumn, **oak**. leaves change to a rich golden colour, but the visual splendour is short-lived as they soon fall*

Redwing *(below) are annual visitors from Scandinavia. Members of the thrush family, they arrive in force in October-November and depart in February, feeding first on berries then on worms and snails*

The earliest overwintering waterfowl to turn up, in October, and the last to leave, usually in March-April, **tufted ducks** are on the increase, with maxima on the Mill Pond of around 30. While the species breeds in many parts of Britain, the local birds have probably come from Scandinavia or Russia

The shortage of small rodents in the vicinity of the Mole is far from ideal for the **kestrel**, which feeds mainly on voles and mice, catching them after using a characteristic hovering flight

CHAPTER 5
Winter

None of you will bid the winter come
To thrust his icy finger in my maw;
Nor let my kingdom's rivers take their course
Through my burn'd bosom; nor entreat the north
To make his bleak winds kiss my parched lips
And comfort me with cold.

WILLIAM SHAKESPEARE, King John

The **pochard**, a diving duck, is a consistent feature at the Mill Pond throughout the winter, departing in early March. They tend to come back, too – this female returned every year from 1991 to 1995. Most of those wintering in Britain breed in central Europe

Roe deer live in small family units for much of the year but during the winter larger herds can gather, containing anything up to a dozen members. The group below, with typically superb camouflage, is pictured on the boundary between the Common Meadow and Randalls Park Crematorium

The **nuthatch** is normally one of our sleekest
year-round residents, but after a bath even the most
stylish can look a little ruffled. Able to move both up
and down trees in search of food due to an
adaptation of the feet, they can be observed around
the islands near Thorncroft Bridge

Winter rain can inundate the Mole's floodplain, including at the Common Meadow

*The **grey squirrel** (below) is less numerous near the river than in more wooded areas, but is still a familiar sight*

*The largest of our three woodpeckers, the **green woodpecker**, is twice the size of the lesser spotted and half as big again as the great spotted. It has a longer tongue than the other two varieties, and uses this to feed mainly on ants, although bark-dwelling insects are also taken. The Common Meadow is a favoured site*

Delightful ice shapes can result when sub-zero temperatures follow flooding on the Common Meadow

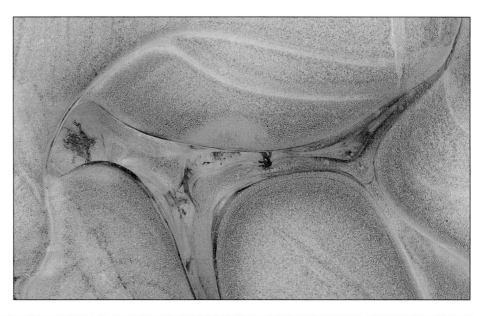

A large duck from the sawbill family, the **goosander** *(below) is increasing as a wintering species, with regular appearances on the Mole and occasional visits to the Mill Pond. This is a juvenile or an adult female; adult males are mainly black and white. Though goosanders breed in Scotland, wintering birds seem to hail from Scandinavia or Russia*

The **siskin** *is one of the bonniest and most abundant winter visitors in good years, with a maximum count of over 100 in a single alder tree near the business park along Riverside Walk in January 1994. Seed eaters from the finch family, they breed mainly in Scotland*

Hidden Jewels

In recent years **gadwall** *(opposite) have been regular at the Mill Pond from December to early March, and their numbers are growing, with a maximum of 12. This reflects a nationwide boost for the species, which breeds chiefly in eastern Europe*

The Mill Pond on a bright, cold February morning

*The plumage of the **starling** is best appreciated in sun, when the full colour and gloss shine out. Ready but not tuneful communicators, they are found practically everywhere, increasing in numbers in winter due to a sizeable influx from the continent*

While the Mill Pond has an excellent record as a breeding site for **swans** (above), icy weather brings problems not experienced on the river. In prolonged cold snaps the residents may even have to move on to the Mole for a spell

The Guildford line railway bridge from Riverside Walk

The **robin** is widespread, popular and seen on many Christmas cards, but due to intense territoriality there is usually little sign of peace and goodwill between them. In winter the feathers are fluffed up to conserve heat

The **little grebe** (below), or dabchick, is just 27cm long and not always easily located due to a tendency to dive for cover at the slightest danger. The species, which feeds on small fish, water insects and snails, breeds along the river and at the Mill Pond

Although **water rail** (right) no longer breed at the Mill Pond, at least one is present most winters. Like moorhens, they are from the crake family and are tremendously secretive. The best chance of a glimpse comes in bitter weather, when they are forced into the open to feed

The **sparrowhawk** (opposite) feeds on other birds and has made a good comeback since the '60s when, due to the effects of pesticides, only a handful bred in the county. Now one or two pairs nest near Leatherhead annually. This is a male, photographed from the front window of the author's flat on a wet day in February

Hoar frosts caused by freezing fog are relatively rare in Mole Valley. They repay close study when they occur, due to the delicate dusting of ice given to virtually all foliage, including these **dog rose** leaves

Hidden Jewels

Brown or grey and with a dry, warty skin, **common toads** are mainly terrestrial, and are nocturnal in their habits. They breed at the Mill Pond in March, producing black, stringy spawn, unlike the bulkier, close-packed frog-spawn

Mute swans clashing over territory is a sure sign of the advent of spring. Fights, which exceptionally can last an hour and result in death for one of the combatants, are between cobs and are always a last resort. The resident cob usually wins

CHAPTER 6

Shaping the Future

Predictions are best left to palmists but one does not need to be a romany to work out what might happen to the River Mole if things go wrong in the next 20 years or so. The knife-edge on which the wildlife lives even now has been commented on in Chapter 1, and far from diminishing, the pressure is likely to increase.

Given sufficient resources, the protection of essential habitats – including river-banks, riffles and pools, and river-bed gravels – can be achieved, and various useful measures undertaken. These include coppicing or pollarding riverside trees, managing neglected woodland, reprofiling banks to improve habitat diversity, reinstating lost landscape features such as hedgerows, and planting trees to create a balance of open and shaded habitats. The River Mole Catchment Landscape Assessment, commissioned by the National Rivers Authority in 1993, put the cost of these and other works in the Leatherhead-Fetcham area at just over £64,000. The estimated cost for all the 14 'target areas' of the Mole covered by the Assessment came to nearly £1.5 million. Natural nuisances – for example, Himalayan balsam, overgrazing, and illegally released exotic wildlife – might also be dealt with, though the ever-increasing damage to native fauna in southern England from the American signal crayfish, for one, suggests confidence in easy solutions could be misplaced.

There is no great cause for confidence about non-natural nuisances, which fall under the broad umbrella of catchment development and include Gatwick and Heathrow Airports, population growth, road construction and industry. Farming could be included here, as over half the river corridor consists of pasture or mixed farmland. On the whole, though, this does not involve intensive working, and as farmers collectively are becoming more and more aware of the importance of the environment, it is reasonable to see the activity as of much less significance than the others. A further reason for saying this is that although farm waste used to be a fairly serious problem in the upper reaches of the river, and herbicides, pesticides and fertilisers gave cause for concern everywhere, the situation has improved quite dramatically in the last decade. We are some way short of perfection – nutrients, headed by phosphates and nitrates, still affect the river through run-off – but of the 48 major or significant pollution incidents in the catchment during the period 1990-95, only three were agricultural in origin.

With the significance of farming duly reduced in the equation, the next three sections focus on contentious and genuinely worrying aspects of development, both generally and with particular reference to the river.

TRANSPORT
Received opinion tells us that those who

oppose development in the 1990s are effectively sponsoring economic stagnation, while those who support it are sponsoring environmental degradation. There are elements of truth in both criticisms because, as has often been observed, truth is rarely black and white but rather an infinite mass of shifting greys.

Up to a point the problems dovetail. Airports supposedly need ever easier access, leading directly to road construction, and they also cause increased urban and industrial development. Bigger airports intensify all this. A fifth terminal at Heathrow, or another runway at Gatwick, would have a considerable effect on Surrey. Monetary wealth would undoubtedly be created but at a major cost to the environment. There would be more people – calculations for Heathrow are for an increase from 35 million to 80 million passengers per annum. There would be more planes, by far the worst form of transport for primary energy consumption and emission of carbon dioxide. There would be more cars – an estimated additional 46,000 vehicles leaving Heathrow each day by 2016. There would be more noise, more fumes, more pollution, increased chemical run-off into waterways, greater demand for water, and further destruction and fragmentation of protected habitats.

As regards Gatwick, the maximum allowable quantity of treated trade effluent going into the Mole is already 70,850 cubic metres per day, and there are six balancing ponds collecting site drainage and contaminated water for discharge. A new lagoon has helped lessen the immediate impact by receiving polluted water from the largest balancing pond and eventually discharging it to the Crawley sewage treatment works, but diversion of the contents of the other ponds is important too. An extra runway would surely increase the scale of discharges, including those of de-icing chemicals, which contribute significantly to water quality problems.

There is no firm evidence that any genuine need for larger airports exists, and the same criticism applies to traffic and the building of more and ever wider roads, even though such development is seen by its supporters as eco-

nomically essential. In one memorable instance their arguments were rebutted by the Confederation of British Industry – scarcely a force for stagnation – which commented that the Department of Transport's plans for the M25 in the early 1990s were as relevant to the British economy as the Sinclair C5.

What exactly the roads lobby has as its vision of the future is debatable, though one element seems to be the conviction that building more roads reduces congestion, when the facts suggest otherwise. Taken to logical extremes, a policy of perpetual growth and construction would allow for little but tarmac, concrete and the incessant throb of the internal combustion engine. And growth, it seems, is inevitable judged on the official forecast – one which should cause a shudder to go down everyone's spine – that traffic levels in Surrey will rise by at least 50% over the next 10 years. This in a county which, according to Surrey County Council's Transport Forum, already has twice the average number of households in the south-east with two or more cars. A county in which traffic levels on motorways and 'A' roads are already twice the national average. And a county in which 90% of the residents who travel to work by car travel alone.

A nightmare? Yes, but one that looks to have a favourite's chance of coming true, largely because of the prevailing mentality which sees vehicle ownership and use as inalienable rights, almost as sacrosanct as, say, the right of self-defence. Individuals who question this notion are often regarded as anti-social, when in fact it is those who never trouble to think carefully about why they are spending time behind the steering wheel, and what effect the action is having, who are closer to being guilty of that sin. Only a fool would argue that modern society could function adequately or comfortably with no motor vehicles, but common sense tells us it is undesirable and far from logical for current traffic levels to increase by 50%. Such a change will do nobody any good and, far from boosting economic growth, is much more likely to put the brakes on due to the sheer inefficiency excess traffic involves and the damage it causes. (Current estimates are that congestion costs the UK economy £20 billion each year, which may rise to £40 billion by the year 2005.)

Nor is the damage restricted to the environment in broad terms. While an increase in the number of verges and banks can benefit some insects and rodents, together with their predators, roads tend to act as ecological barriers, blocking natural corridors. Their construction can destroy habitats not only on site but in areas many miles away where the required aggregates are quarried in bulk. Road building also changes the wildlife found along any route by affecting light, humidity and soil nutrients, while the resulting air and noise pollution can reduce the overall level of insects and songbirds. Informed estimates of the numbers of creatures killed on British roads each year are: barn owls 5,000; badgers 47,000; foxes 100,000; hedgehogs 100,000; toads one million.

According to some research, the average British car owner spends an estimated 600 hours, or 25 days, a year driving in heavy traffic. Even if there is a suspicion with such a large figure that the researcher's definition of 'heavy' might have been a shade broad, the feeling remains 'what a waste'. And what an even bigger waste if a 50% increase occurred. How much better if some, at least, of that time could be spent in enjoying the environment rather than in an activity which threatens habitats and their residents, and does nothing for anyone's peace of mind.

No-one can blame local authorities for not doing their best. Surrey County Council and local district councils, notably Mole Valley, campaigned vigorously against the scheme to widen parts of the M25 to 14 lanes, and SCC's Transport Plan is certainly environmentally friendly with its limits on road building, introduction of company transport plans and encouragement of non peak-time travel among other policies. Perhaps the Plan could go deeper, but it does at least scratch the surface, and scratching this surface is decidedly superior to applying polish. Further scratches or, even better, gouges would come if car owners and drivers started seriously exercising their grey matter about the implications of how

and why they use their vehicles. Also, they would come if Governments started paying attention to what informed bodies such as the Royal Commission on Environmental Pollution tell them about the unacceptable consequences of excess traffic and relentless road construction.

American-style car pools would assist, as would using smaller, more fuel-efficient cars, and not using cars at all for short journeys. Three radical changes, backed by a wide range of conservation bodies, would help even more. First, the creation of a sustainable, integrated national transport system – theoretically the perfect inducement to drive less, be it with cars, with vans or with lorries. Secondly, stopping the way road transport is relatively underpriced, in the sense that the cost is not proportionate to the expense the action imposes on society or the environment. Thirdly, changing land-use planning policies in order to reduce the long-term need to travel using motorised transport.

Yet No. 1 appears to have been dealt a blow by the deregulation of bus services and the privatisation of the railways, while No. 2 and, to a lesser extent, No. 3 tend to come up against a brick wall – Government, commercial and public coolness. Sadly, as far as Governments are concerned the reason for slashing billion-pound road programmes, and for increasing road fund tax and taxation on petroleum products, is never genuine principle or care for the environment. No, the reason is financial expediency, and so long as the strength and health of the car industry continues to be viewed as a prime indicator of Britain's economic well-being, nothing is likely to alter.

URBAN GROWTH

Traffic is a national malaise, albeit one with a greater impact in Surrey than in most places. Moving from the general to the specific, further development within the Mole catchment is hardly likely to be beneficial. Due to its impermeable nature, the local strata would make the river 'flashy' and very responsive to rainfall even without input from other sources. The strata, though, is 'assisted', for while rain that falls on fields is released gradually into rivers and streams, rain that falls on tarmac and concrete goes straight into the waterways via surface drains.

One consequence of this is a shorter-term but often higher level of flooding, and when this happens in April-May, nesting birds – especially kingfishers, mute swans, little grebes and moorhens – suffer accordingly. It is rare for kingfishers to fledge their first brood on the Mole, and no cygnets have hatched and fledged on the river around Leatherhead for at least 10 years. One pair of swans lost four nests containing a total of 20 eggs near Leatherhead Bridge in 1990 and 1991.

The way in which the NRA liaised with local planning authorities to protect the catchment from unsuitable development has helped to a degree. The Environment Agency is continuing this responsibility. Equally, it is hardly encouraging that the population of Crawley is expected to rise from 89,000 to nearly 105,000 by 2006. Or that social changes leading to a steady increase in the number of one- and two-person households are perceived as automatically necessitating the construction of an additional 4.4 million new housing units nationwide over the next 20 years. The Replacement Surrey Structure Plan, for instance, contains an allocation of an extra 1,300 dwellings at Horley between 2001 and 2006, and the potential for another 1,300 thereafter. This is bound to affect the Mole.

People need employment and that activity demands industrial development at one level or another. Further growth would inevitably increase the danger of an acute pollution incident and if, for some reason, the emergency services were unable to cope, the results could well be catastrophic. People also need support services, and place immense pressure on facilities for disposing of both solid and liquid waste. Around 575,000 tonnes of solid waste are generated in the Mole catchment each year, with only 10% recycled. If this is a miserable indictment of modern society, even worse is the fact that the remaining 90% has to be put in landfills in Surrey and West Sussex, including an unlined one at Redhill with the capacity to

swallow an anticipated six million tonnes over the next 15 years. The landfill tax introduced at the end of 1995 – £7 per tonne on household waste, £2 per tonne on construction waste – should force a rethink about recycling and disposal, and it is encouraging that the recycling target for the Mole Valley district for the year 2000 is 25%. Yet little is likely to happen overnight, and taxing an activity can spawn fresh difficulties, in this instance a possible increase in illegal 'fly tipping'.

WASTE WATER

Solid waste can affect groundwater if landfill sites are unlined but generally it has much less immediate impact on waterways than liquid waste, or sewage, which is the strong second element behind oil and chemicals in the catalogue of causes of pollution incidents on the Mole mentioned in Chapter 1. There is, in fact, what may be termed a love-hate relationship between the Mole and sewage, which in the public sphere concerns the sewage treatment works (STWs) run by Thames Water Utilities Ltd. These works are essential, and given that each of us produces on average 225 litres (50 gallons) of waste water each day, watercourses are the only logical route for discharging the treated effluent. A lot of liquid is involved, and this is the 'love' element, since STWs help the Mole considerably in times of drought by providing at least 50%, and sometimes up to 80%, of the flow. That was one reason why the river stayed in good shape during the almost rainless summer of 1995.

At first sight, the treated sewage effluent discharge consents of the nine main STWs on the Mole and its tributaries through the 1990s are grim. Granted and regulated in quality as well as quantity by the Environment Agency, they total a maximum of nearly 310,000 cubic metres per day, over half of which is discharged between the river's source and Leatherhead town. (One cubic metre equals 1,000 litres.) The figures would make much grislier reading if the sewage was raw, rather than treated and of officially high quality. In fact, in wet weather or storm conditions dilute settled sewage is occasionally discharged direct into the Mole, and there can also be foul sewer/pumping station overflows.

The good news is that Thames Water Utilities is at last addressing these two problems through the installation of fine screens and provision of storm water storage facilities. Even treated sewage is 'oxygen hungry', though, and lack of that element is one sign of a sick river, as well as one of the principal causes of shortfalls in wildlife on waterways across the whole country. Admittedly, the effluent situation on the Mole is nothing like so bad as on some British rivers. Chemical sampling shows the percentage of dissolved oxygen – an index of purity – is lowest nearest to STWs, in the region of 60%, compared with up to 75% further downstream. Officially, according to what is called the Water Quality Objective scale, 60% is a pretty fair rating, but it is worth noting this comment by the NRA towards the end of 1995: "The effects of treated sewage effluents and other human impacts continue to restrict biological diversity [in the Mole]."

Chemical worries over sewage are, if anything, exceeded by bacteriological ones. Tests by Mole Valley District Council at four sites in 1993 revealed that in every instance out of 16 the Mole failed the Acceptable Standard of the relevant EC Directive on coliform organisms. (Coliform organisms are bacteria which inhabit the intestinal tract of humans and animals and may cause disease.) In seven cases, the samples failed the much broader Imperative Standard. At the Stepping Stones, downstream of the Dorking STW, the sample was 800 times above the Acceptable Standard in August 1993, leading Mole Valley District Council's Chief Environmental Health Officer John Tiffney to describe the Mole as "bacteriologically filthy". A proportion of the impurity at the four sites could have been caused by factors beyond the influence of Thames Water Utilities, such as farm animals, horses, dogs and leakages from rural cesspits and from septic tanks, but the high level of the returns nearest to Dorking STW looks pretty conclusive.

No British or EC rules are being broken by Thames Water Utilities, which is a responsible company. It has been investing considerable sums in upgrading STWs, and will continue doing that under its 10-year Asset Management Plan to 2005. All STWs in Mole Valley provide at least secondary biological treatment, which means they meet the quality requirements of EC Urban Waste Water Treatment Directive 91/1271/EEC. But – and it is a fair-sized but – that Directive, which will come into force only in 2004, does not include *as the norm* additional tertiary treatment to meet bacteriological standards. Indeed, remarkable as this may seem, "there are no statutory bacteriological standards yet available for coliform bacteria levels in rivers that can be used to assess health risks associated with river water contact" (NRA 1995). For a company with shareholders to answer to, this absence of an absolute legal requirement effectively makes the introduction of beneficial but expensive chlorination equipment at best problematical and at worst inconceivable.

The plus side, as far as environmentalists are concerned, is that in running water, rather than still, bacteriological impurities are liable to have a greater impact on people than on wildlife. Humans, unlike fauna, do not need to go into the River Mole to live, to find food and drink, to breed or to 'move house', so it is not exactly an overwhelming disaster if they are obliged to avoid direct contact. They at least have a choice. Yet high levels of impurities are not acceptable, either in themselves or in the way they influence public opinion. If the residents of Mole Valley and elsewhere believe the Mole is filthy, they may start giving up on the river, and may start viewing it with less excitement and delight than it deserves. Indifference is no recipe for a secure future for the environment. The best way of ensuring such a future, as regards sewage anyway, is first to ensure there are no acute pollution incidents, and secondly to make treated effluent even cleaner – whatever the financial cost.

SUSTAINABLE DEVELOPMENT

Cost has been a recurring element in this chapter. Not quite everything in late 20th century Britain is governed by economic imperatives but most things, it seems, are. Those who lobby for non-sustainable development invariably use an equation involving financial values and costs, and material benefits. However, the premise lacks universal or even specific validity because it discounts other values and costs, notably those of natural habitats. And the latter, being of inestimable value physically, morally and aesthetically, weaken if not obliterate any purely cash-based arguments put up against them.

Economic growth and the creation of wealth are desirable in any society, but when they come at a progressively greater cost to the environment it is not just modern Luddites who should cry 'foul' and argue that striking a balance is essential. The only acceptable principle should be that for any development, be it a new road, urban growth or a new factory, *all* the costs must be weighed up. Nor is it good enough merely to pay lip service to this concept, as the Department of Transport has made a habit of doing. The Department is supposed to take account of environmental impact when assessing whether a road should be built but in practice it has consistently managed to avoid this. Local action is insufficient; genuine commitment at a high level is required.

On the face of it, middle ground between the polarised camps of developers and environmentalists is about as easy to find as a salmon in the Mole, yet some hope lies in the notion of sustainable development. This forms an intrinsic part of the blueprint put forward at the 1992 Earth Summit in Rio, and of Agenda 21, which aims to put those Rio ideals into action. Stripped of some of the vague and trendy elements which have surrounded it from the start, sustainable development is, in essence, economically viable, environmentally sound and socially acceptable. It is development which guarantees an absence of deterioration across the board, including ecologically.

Quite how this will be organised or safeguarded, how pious hopes will be turned into glorious reality, remains unclear. Elected bodies generally appear to be beginning to appreciate the true value of the natural world and the importance of protecting it. This is not only because environmental issues receive consistent publicity and because public opinion has a distinct green tinge, leading to serious consequences in PR terms if nature is trampled on. There is genuine concern as well. Similarly, while self-interest – in other words, fear of negative publicity – may be a prime reason for caution among companies when the environment enters the picture, conviction and principle can, and in places do, play a part.

Locally, prospects for sustainable development are reasonable, but on a wider basis, in the ever-expanding global economy, a change in human nature may be necessary for the success of the scheme. Such changes occur infrequently. Businesses compete and are out to make money, and if one – here, in the rest of Europe or anywhere else – steals a march by not behaving 'sustainably', will its rivals sit back and act nobly and responsibly? Only a supreme optimist would bet on it, as such an approach might be tantamount to committing commercial suicide. The drawback with sustainable development is that it is likely to cost all of us something, so public enthusiasm is less than assured. Winning hearts and minds when there is a material price to be paid is seldom easy, yet if nothing is done, the ultimate cost to mankind is going to be considerably greater.

RIVER MOLE CATCHMENT MANAGEMENT PLAN

Closely connected with the Agenda 21 principles, and of major local significance, is the River Mole Catchment Management Plan formulated by the Environment Agency after wide consultation in 1995-96. The aim of such plans is to "protect areas of unspoilt natural beauty and pure waters and to protect the water environment within the principles of sustainable development and environmental capacity." In keeping with the philosophy of Local Agenda 21 – working together as a community to ensure today's lifestyles do not ruin the chances of succeeding generations, and to forge a better, environmentally sound future – the Plan sees community involvement as fundamental. It is "the cornerstone of this approach to managing the local water environment, not only by raising awareness but also by promoting active participation in environmental enhancement."

The initial Action Plan, the first in an intended series, homes in on most of the problems, real and potential, outlined in this chapter. It proposes possible ways of counteracting them spread over five years, constantly monitored, with a full review commencing in June 1998. Preventing pollution and improving water quality are, quite rightly, at the top of the agenda, but no-one with a realistic turn of mind would expect fine intentions to be as simple to achieve in practice as they are to write about in a plan. One can expect dialogues of the deaf between interested parties on a few issues, and consent for action may not be obtained easily in every case.

Suspicious observers may have qualms regarding the 'split personality' of the NRA/Environment Agency, under which these organisations' aims and strategies have included the promotion of both "the conservation of aquatic flora and fauna" and "the use of water and associated land for recreational purposes". These two are not always compatible, for the simple reason that increased public access and conservation can be uncomfortable bedfellows. One aim of the Plan is to "investigate the opportunities for increased navigation and water-based recreation" on the Mole, while another identifies "the need to protect important in-stream and river corridor habitats". Despite this potential inconsistency, the NRA/Environment Agency's record through the 1990s suggests the vital balance between enjoyment and responsible custodianship will be maintained. Unquestionably, if it comes to a direct clash, responsible custodianship should win. Well-organised education is one way of getting this message across to the widest possible audience, and is covered to an extent in the Plan, chiefly in connection with pollution and litter.

More worrying, in an era when cutbacks in Government expenditure seem to be the norm, is the question of the funding of proposed improvements and actions in Catchment Management Plans nationwide. After all, in one respect the Mole is not unique, because there are 20 other catchments within the Thames region, all covered by Management Plans or Local Environment Agency Plans. The Thames, too, while second only to the Severn in length among British rivers, is merely one among many watercourses across the country. When the money comes to be handed out each year, the environment rarely ranks as high as its supporters would like it to – the threat of closure hanging over a number of city farms, and the withdrawal of funding for the Living Churchyard Grant, are two examples of this. Voluntary groups can help in small matters but to manage catchments effectively requires considerable resources. Additional funding, rather than the status quo or reductions, may well be needed to achieve the Environment Agency's objectives for the Mole once all have been precisely costed. One which has not been costed, but which is accorded high priority in the Plan, is the implementation of the recommendations contained in the River Mole Catchment Landscape Assessment mentioned at the start of this chapter. If implemented in its entirety, the Assessment will involve the expenditure of not thousands but hundreds of thousands of pounds – as much as all the actions already costed put together.

Despite these fears, cautious optimism is justified. The Plan contains a number of proposals for enhancement, among them maintenance at Leatherhead, including landscape, conservation and recreation management. This is costed at £25,000, and is accorded only medium priority. Encouragingly, though, a study of the River Mole through Leatherhead by the Environment Agency, Mole Valley District Council and Surrey County Council started towards the end of 1996. This study covers such aspects as safeguarding and enhancing the nature conservation interest of the area through co-ordinated management; ensuring habitat diversity; the removal or screening of eyesores; and the provision of appropriate interpretive material.

This close linking of local authorities with the Environment Agency is very positive, and indicates that the Catchment Management Plan should dovetail neatly with the good work already being done by the Lower Mole

Countryside Management Project, and with Mole Valley District Council's Nature Conservation Strategy. The underlying principle of the Strategy is "protecting and enhancing the district's heritage of wild flora and fauna, together with their habitats". The dedicated professionalism of the Environment Agency's employees lends additional encouragement, and all other things being equal, the Plan and its successors should prevent some potential difficulties becoming a reality into the 21st century. They should also give the river a fighting chance of successfully combating those which do arise. For that reason, these official statements of intent deserve to be supported not only by the general public but also by the business community.

A greater sense of awareness of the river and, as the Environment Agency puts it, "more responsible citizenship", will certainly be welcome, especially if they lead to less litter being discarded on the banks of the Mole and in the water. At present, anything portable seems fair game to be hurled in, notably supermarket trolleys and traffic cones. Perhaps this provides some spurious form of 'street credibility', or perhaps those who behave like this either do not know what beauty is, or are hostile to it. At least the worst results of their behaviour, unlike those of polluters and unsympathetic developers, can be sorted out by ordinary citizens prepared to collect litter voluntarily.

Local Agenda 21 should provide a fillip for this and other direct actions. Among these, the wise and economic use of water is likely to become progressively more important. The gravity of the drought situation in the United Kingdom is sometimes exaggerated by those unable or unwilling to look beyond the ends of their noses. Equally, in various parts of the world increasing demand for diminishing stocks poses one of the greatest threats to wild water environments as well as human existence, and even here there is no excuse for wasting water or taking it for granted. It is too precious a resource to be used cavalierly, so there is little cause for pride in the fact that the daily consumption of water per household in the Sutton and East Surrey Water plc area is 20% above the national average.

Above all, everyone should realise that the priority with the Mole, and the area where resources need to be concentrated initially, is in making sure the river survives as a thriving wildlife habitat. To this end, improvements aimed at recreating conditions and habitats that existed 50 or more years ago, such as wet meadows, should have undivided attention devoted to them only when the future is secure. Any premature action will be a waste, on which front it may be misguided to think about spending time and money on, say, reintroducing the otter when creatures already on the premises face less than ideal circumstances. Getting things right for the present residents is the first duty, and doing that should naturally make it more feasible to do our bit for former ones as well, thereby increasing biodiversity. It would certainly be a help if the Common Meadow and the area around it were managed properly for wildlife. The designation of the Meadow as common land severely restricts any possibilities for development. However, the current policy of inaction can be almost as harmful as development. Tremendous benefit would be gained if this policy were replaced by one that is vigorous and environmentally sound. The Common Meadow deserves nothing less.

FETCHAM MILL POND – MANAGEMENT

By contrast with the river, Fetcham Mill Pond faces no dangers from pollution, run-off or effluent, and while ponds all over Britain have been disappearing at an alarming rate during the last 30 years, this one is safe. The fact that fishing and boating are banned, and public access is restricted to just a sixth of the perimeter, has enabled the emergent vegetation which is vital for wildlife to flourish. The Pond has not been neglected, in the sense of being allowed to dry out or fill with vegetation and litter. However, improvements could undoubtedly be made to guarantee an even brighter future.

Sutton and East Surrey Water plc is highly efficient and successful, providing award-winning drinking water and the lowest losses through leakages of any water company in Britain, but it appears to be walking rather than running down the path of conservation. Yes, it owns a number of rich habitats, is a corporate member of Surrey Wildlife Trust and the Kent Trust for Nature Conservation (which runs the nature reserve at Bough Beech Reservoir), and applies sound 'green' principles in running the business. Yet, oddly, S&ESW does not have a specialist nature conservation officer.

The lack of positive management at the Mill Pond possibly reflects this absence, though it is not always a case of too little being done. On the contrary, too much is sometimes done, notably in the way of regular mowing of the 'improved' – an ecological misnomer – grassland around the Pond. Tidiness is an admirable quality in a company, but more in administration and finance than in environmental care. Surely nature's tidiness, managed efficiently, is preferable, providing it does nothing to impair the provision of water to the public, which is S&ESW's duty and greatest priority.

It is hard to believe efficiency or anything else would be impaired by cutting the grass not monthly through the spring and summer, which is the present practice, but just once a year in late-summer, hay meadow style. This might well encourage a dazzling show of wild flowers, and the butterflies to go with them. At the moment such butterfly food-plants as bird's-foot trefoil, Yorkshire fog, common sorrel and cocksfoot, along with the attractive brooklime, all appear, only to get eliminated in their prime. Even a small colony of cowslips – uncommon locally – does not automatically receive immunity from the blades, since a third of them were mown down in 1995 despite being carefully marked out by me acting as voluntary warden.

Among the numerous people who walk along by, and take delight in, the Mill Pond, who would not rather see a colourful mix of flowers and grasses than a tidy but barren green desert of the type visible in the spring and summer of 1996? Apart from anything else, this relatively simple form of management might encourage skylarks to breed. The species, in decline nationally due principally to modern farming methods, has nested in small numbers in the field to the north-west of the Mill Pond in

recent years. Disturbance there is likelier than within the fence around the Pond. While on the subject of the field, the Mole Valley Local Plan contains the seed of a scheme to turn it into an informal recreation area. Following on from that, Fetcham's 'Community Together' Local Agenda 21 programme proposed creating a nature conservation area on the site. By all accounts the owners, S&ESW, are opposed to this suggestion, due to possible future "operational requirements". The field will almost certainly be left under agriculture for the time being, but that itself makes the location a reasonable unofficial nature conservation area, always providing the current non-intensive farming methods continue to be applied.

Returning to the Mill Pond, positive management would also benefit the birds and dragonflies that use the duct running from the pumping station towards the fire station. Snipe in particular is not a common mid-Surrey species even in winter, and anything which can be done to assist this welcome visitor should be done. Some improvements could be effected to the Pond itself in line with recommendations made by the Surrey Wildlife Trust officer who surveyed the location as a potential Site of Nature Conservation Importance in June 1993. These include allowing emergent vegetation communities to expand, and re-sculpturing the contours of the island, creating a sinuous margin with gradual waterside gradients. A systematic survey of invertebrates, amphibians and fish would also be most useful in providing data and in checking whether certain important species – the great crested newt, for instance – are present.

It is difficult to imagine that S&ESW's shareholders, for all their understandable interest in good financial returns, could fail to see the potential benefits of a slightly more sophisticated policy by the company regarding natural habitats, flora and fauna. Good publicity is worth its weight in gold and has a useful knock-on effect on the stock of any organisation. Given the withering fire under which privatised service industries have been coming in recent years, such a development by S&ESW presumably would be an appealing prospect, the more so because the necessary investment in time and money would be far from excessive. All that is required is a slight change in perspective.

Time will tell whether such a change occurs. In the interim, those who care about the Mill Pond and, more particularly, the River Mole can hope for improvements. Better still, they can press for them as individuals, through residents' associations, or within any of the numerous groups which actively work to protect and benefit the environment. Among these are Surrey Wildlife Trust, Leatherhead & District Countryside Protection Society and the Mole Valley Conservation Volunteers. Pressure to protect habitats can and should be placed on local authorities, on statutory bodies such as the Environment Agency, and, where necessary, on businesses if their policies pose a threat.

One thing is certain. Nobody should take anything for granted in admiring natural wonders, local or national, for no-one can say which, if any, may all too soon have the life squeezed out of them. In the final analysis, inattention to such jewels would amount to betrayal, and even casual interest may be insufficient. The only near-guarantee lies in eternal vigilance, which has always been the price of beauty as well as of liberty.

Further Reading

W.S. Atkins (Planning Consultants), River Mole Catchment Landscape Assessment, National Rivers Authority 1993

Birds of Conservation Concern, RSPB 1996

M. Birkhead & C. Perrins, The Mute Swan, Croom Helm 1986

D. Boag, Kingfisher, Blandford Press 1982

Breaking Point – the RSPB's policy on transport and biodiversity, RSPB 1995

G.A. Collins, Butterflies of Surrey, Surrey Wildlife Trust 1995

J. Dallaway, Views in the Vicarage of Leatherhead, London 1821

G. Douglas, Recent Changes in Bird Populations, Proceedings of Leatherhead and District Local History Society 1951

J. Drewett, Nature of Surrey, Barracuda Books 1987

P. Fioratti, Kingfisher, Harper Collins 1992

R.S.R. Fitter, London's Natural History, Collins 1945

R. Fitter & R. Manuel, Field Guide to Freshwater Life, Collins 1986

P. Follett, Dragonflies of Surrey, Surrey Wildlife Trust 1996

S.E.D. Fortescue, Leatherhead in Old Picture Postcards, European Library 1988

S. Harris, Urban Foxes, Whittet Books 1986

J. Hillier, Old Surrey Water-mills, Skeffington & Son 1951

J. Lewarne, Fetcham Cutt-Mill, Proceedings of Leatherhead and District Local History Society 1970

J.E. Lousley, Flora of Surrey, David & Charles 1976

A. McGeeney, A Complete Guide to British Dragonflies, Jonathan Cape 1986

Mole Valley Local Plan – Deposit Version, Mole Valley District Council 1996

Natural World magazine, The Wildlife Trusts, various 1991-95

Nature Line magazine, Surrey Wildlife Trust, various 1991-95

The New Rivers and Wildlife Handbook, RSPB/NRA 1994

J.S. Ogilvy, A Pilgrimage in Surrey, Routledge 1914

E. Parker, Highways and Byways of Surrey, Robert Hale 1908

D. Parr (editor), Birds of Surrey, Batsford 1972

River Corridor Surveys – The River Mole and Its Tributaries, University of Sheffield 1992

River Mole Catchment Management Plan Consultation Report, NRA 1996

River Mole Catchment Management Plan – Action Plan, Environment Agency 1997

River Mole Fisheries Survey, Thames Water 1986

River Mole Fisheries Survey, NRA 1989

Royal Commission on Environmental Pollution – Transport and the Environment, HMSO 1994

A.T. Ruby, The Leatherhead River, Proceedings of Leatherhead and District Local History Society 1964

P. A. Tarplee, A Guide to the Industrial History of Mole Valley District, Surrey Industrial History Group 1995

E. Vardey (editor), History of Leatherhead, De Valery 1988

P.A.L. Vine, Surrey Waterways, Middleton Press 1988

Wildlife & Countryside Act, HMSO 1981

Species Checklist and Index

This checklist lays no claim to be comprehensive other than in the sense that it includes all the major species to have met my gaze between 1987 and 1997. Other wildlife watchers should be able to add different species, particularly bats, and with luck, as the years go by, I'll be able to add a few myself. 1995 brought weasel and yellow-winged darter dragonfly, 1996 curlew, red-eyed damselfly and clouded yellow butterfly, and 1997 began with a smew. That is part of the delight of nature watching. Not included are tame aliens, such as Muscovy duck, and presumed escapes, such as a male wood duck seen in October 1996. Names are given in English and Latin, and figures are textual references, with bold denoting a picture.

MAMMALS

Badger *(Meles meles)* 14
Bat, brown long-eared *(Plecotus auritus)*
Bat, pipistrelle *(Pipistrellus pipistrellus)*
Deer, roe *(Capreolus capreolus)* 14, **46, 68**
Fox, red *(Vulpes vulpes)* 14, **29, 42**
Hedgehog *(Erinaceus europaeus)*
Mink, American *(Mustela vison)* 12, 13
Mole *(Talpa europaea)* 13
Mouse, house *(Mus musculus)*
Mouse, wood *(Apodemus sylvaticus)*
Rabbit *(Oryctolagus cuniculus)* 14
Rat, brown *(Rattus norvegicus)* 16
Shrew, common *(Sorex araneus)*
Shrew, water *(Neomys fodiens)*
Squirrel, grey *(Sciurus carolinensis)* **70**
Stoat *(Mustela erminea)* 14
Vole, water *(Arvicola terrestris)* 13
Weasel *(Mustela nivalis)* 14

BIRDS

Blackbird *(Turdus merula)*
Blackcap *(Sylvia atricapilla)* 10, 13
Brambling *(Fringilla montifringilla)*
Bullfinch *(Pyrrhula pyrrhula)* 12, 14
Bunting, reed *(Emberiza schoeniclus)* 12, 16
Chaffinch *(Fringilla coelebs)*
Chiffchaff *(Phylloscopus collybita)* 16
Coot *(Fulica atra)* 16, **24, 50**

Cormorant *(Phalacrocorax carbo)* 14
Crow, carrion *(Corvus corone corone)*
Cuckoo *(Cuculus canorus)*
Curlew *(Numenius arquata)*
Dove, collared *(Streptopelia decaocto)*
Dove, stock *(Columba oenas)*
Duck, mandarin *(Aix galericulata)* 12, 13, **53**
Duck, tufted *(Aythya fuligula)* 14, 16, **65**
Dunnock *(Prunella modularis)*
Fieldfare *(Turdus pilaris)* 14
Flycatcher, spotted *(Muscicapa striata)* 12, 14
Gadwall *(Anas strepera)* 14, 16, **75**
Goldcrest *(Regulus regulus)* 16
Goldfinch *(Carduelis carduelis)* 14
Goosander *(Mergus merganser)* 14, 16, **72**
Goose, Canada *(Branta canadensis)*
Grebe, great crested *(Podiceps cristatus)* **22**
Grebe, little *(Tachybaptus ruficollis)* 13, 14, 15, 16, **77,** 84
Greenfinch *(Carduelis chloris)* 16
Gull, black-headed *(Larus ridibundus)* 16
Gull, common *(Larus canus)*
Gull, lesser black-backed *(Larus fuscus)*
Gull, herring *(Larus argentatus)*
Heron, grey *(Ardea cinerea)* 13, 14, **30, 51**
Jackdaw *(Corvus monedula)*
Jay *(Garrulus glandarius)* 13

Kestrel *(Falco tinnunculus)* 13, **66**
Kingfisher *(Alcedo atthis)* 10, 13, 14, 15, 16, **25, 56, 57,** 84
Lapwing *(Vanellus vanellus)* 14, 16
Linnet *(Carduelis cannabina)* 16
Magpie *(Pica pica)*
Mallard *(Anas platyrhynchos)* 16, **33**
Martin, house *(Delichon urbica)* 16
Martin, sand *(Riparia riparia)* 16
Merganser, red-breasted *(Mergus serrator)*
Moorhen *(Gallinula chloropus)* 10, 14, 15, **26,** 84
Nuthatch *(Sitta europaea)* **69**
Owl, little *(Athene noctua)* 14
Owl, tawny *(Strix aluco)* 14
Pheasant *(Phasianus colchicus)*
Pigeon, feral *(Columba livia)*
Pipit, meadow *(Anthus pratensis)* 14
Pochard *(Aythya ferina)* 16, **68**
Rail, water *(Rallus aquaticus)* 15, 16, **78**
Redpoll *(Carduelis flammea)* 14
Redshank *(Tringa totanus)*
Redwing *(Turdus iliacus)* 14, **64**
Robin *(Erithacus rubecula)* **77**
Rook *(Corvus frugilegus)* 15
Sandpiper, common *(Actitis hypoleucos)* 14
Sandpiper, green *(Tringa ochropus)* 14
Shoveler *(Anas clypeata)* 16
Siskin *(Carduelis spinus)* 14, **73**
Skylark *(Alauda arvensis)* 12, 16, 89
Smew *(Mergus albellus)* 16

The Photographs

Ideally, nature photography does justice to originals without expecting to improve on them. It is also a vastly better recording method than the old style of using a gun, and a lot of fun to boot, even when it means getting up at 4.30am in the morning to 'shoot' kingfishers. Or when, as happened a few years ago, two police officers descended on my carefully arranged hide following mistaken information that the occupant was a trespassing vagrant.

For the record, details of the photographs in Hidden Jewels follow, showing lens, aperture, shutter speed and film, as far as memory recollects all these. Six different types of 35mm camera were used – Praktica MTL5B, Minolta Dynax 7000i, 8000i and 700SI, Canon EOS100 and EOS5. The abbreviations for films are: K25 (Kodachrome 25), K64 (Kodachrome 64), K200 (Kodachrome 200), F50 (Fujichrome 50), F100 (Fujichrome 100), S100 (Fujichrome Sensia 100) and V (Fujichrome Velvia).

Cover: Mill Pond, 35-105mm, f5.6, 250th, F100

Back cover: Small skipper, 100mm macro, f8, 15th, S100

18: Black-tailed skimmer, 200mm + 2x conv., f11, 60th, V

19: Mill Pond, 24mm, f11, 125th, F100

20: Orange tip, 100mm macro, f8, 30th, K25
Wood garlic, 20-35mm, f5.6, 45th, K64

21: Great spotted woodpecker, 800mm + 1.4x conv., f11, 125th, K200

22: Great crested grebes, 300mm, f8, 125th, K200
Great crested grebe, 300mm + 2x conv., f6.7, 125th, K200

23: Speckled wood, 100mm macro + ringflash, f9.5 auto, F50

24: Swans, 135mm, f5.6, 180th, F100
Coots, 500mm, f8, 250th, K200

25: Kingfisher, 800mm, f9.5, 250th, K200

Minnows, 200mm + polariser, f5.6, 90th, K200

26: Red campion, 20-35, f8, 30th, F100
Moorhen, 500mm, f6.7, 250th, K200

27: Swan & cygnets, 300mm + 1.4x conv., f4.5, 180th, K200
Flooded nest, 135mm, f4, 60th, F100

28: Buttercups, 35-135mm, f8 auto, S100
Web, 100mm macro, f8, 90th, F100

29: Vixen & cub, 800mm, f6.7, 125th, K200
Cubs, 800mm, f6.7 auto, K200

30: Grey heron, 300mm, f4 auto, K64

31: Swan family, 100-300mm, f5.6, 125th, V
Cygnets, 200mm, f4, 250th, K200

32: Mill Pond, 35-105mm, f9.5, 125th, F100

33: Water-crowfoot, 135mm, f8, 30th, K64
Mallard & ducklings, 200mm, f8, 250th, K200

34: Mayfly, 100mm macro + ringflash, f11 auto, F100
Crab spider, 100mm macro + ringflash, f13 auto, F50

35: Banded demoiselle, 100mm macro, f8, 180th, K200

36: Grey wagtail, 800mm, f8 auto, K200

37: Small tortoiseshell caterpillars, 100mm macro, f9.5, 125th, K200

Small tortoiseshell, 100mm macro + ringflash, f11 auto, F100

38: Sedge warbler, 300mm + 2x conv., f6.7, 180th, F100

39: Fetcham Splash, 20-35mm, f8 auto, K25

40: Purple loosestrife, 35-350mm, f8, 15th, V

Common blue butterfly, 100m macro + ringflash, f11 auto, F100

41: White-legged damselfly, 100mm macro, f9.5, 125th, K200

42: Fox cub, 300mm + 1.4x conv., f5.6, 125th, K200

Gatekeeper, 100mm macro + ringflash, f16 auto, F100

43: Common darter, 35-350mm + 12mm tube, f8, 6th, V

44: Greater dodder, 100mm macro, f8, 180th, S100

Swan, 500mm, f6.7, 500th, K200

45: Mill Pond, 20-35mm, f8, 20th, K25

46: Buck roe deer, 200mm + 2x conv., f5.6, 350th, K200

Doe & fawn, 200mm + 2x conv., f4.5, 250th, V

47: Common blue damselflies, 100mm macro, f9.5, 125th, S100

48: Dark bush cricket, 100mm macro + ringflash, f11 auto, F100

Large skipper, 100mm macro + ringflash, f13 auto, F100

49: Garden spider, 100mm macro, f16, 30th, K200

50: Painted lady, 100mm macro + ringflash, f9.5 auto, F100

Coots, 500mm, f8, 350th, K200

51: Grey heron, 300mm + 1.4x conv., f5.6, 90th, K200

52: Ringlet, 100mm macro, f5.6, 60th, K200

Sunset, 70-210mm, f4, 60th, S100

53: Mandarin duck, 300mm + 1.4x conv., f5.6, 180th, K200

Horse chestnut, 35-350mm, f8, 20th, S100

54: Migrant hawkers, 200mm + 2x conv., f9.5, 30th, V

55: Common Meadow, 70-210mm, f9.5, 60th, V

56: Kingfisher, 800mm, f5.6, 125th, K200

57: Kingfishers, 800mm, f11, 20th, K200

58: Rose hips, 35-105mm, f11, 90th, F100

Peacock, 100mm macro + ringflash, f9.5 auto, F100

59: Common darter, 200mm + 25mm tube, f8, 1/2 sec, V

60: Field maple, 70-210mm, f8, 60th, S100

61: Small copper, 100mm macro, f8, 125th, K200

Swans, 24mm, f5.6, 500th, K200

62: Ladybirds, 100mm macro, f9.5 auto, S100

Holly berries, 135m, f8, 180th, F100

63: Brown hawker, 35-350mm, f6.7, 15th, V

64: Oak leaf, 100mm macro, f8 auto, K64

Redwing, 300mm + 2x conv., f8, 250th, K200

65: Tufted ducks, 500mm, f9.5, 125th, K200

66: Kestrel, 500mm, f8, 250th, K200

67: Mill Pond, 24mm, f5.6, 30th, K64

68: Pochard, 300mm + 1.4x conv., f4.5, 180th, K200

Roe deer, 300mm + 1.4x conv., f4 auto, K200

69: Nuthatch, 800mm + 12mm tube, f5.6, 90th, K200

70: River Mole, 20-35mm, f8 auto, V

Grey squirrel, 500mm, f6.7, 180th, K200

71: Green woodpecker, 800mm, f5.6, 30th, K200

72: Ice, 100mm macro, f8 auto, V

Goosander, 800mm, f9.5, 180th, K200

73: Siskin, 800mm, f6.7, 125th, K200

74: Mill Pond, 35-105mm, f8, 45th, V

75: Gadwall, 800mm, f8, 180th, K200

Starling, 300mm, f4.5, 500th, K200

76: Swans, 200mm, f6.7, 125th, K200

River Mole, 24mm, f8, 125th, F100

77: Robin, 300mm + 1.4x conv., f4, 250th, K200

Little grebe, 800mm, f5.6, 90th, K200

78: Sparrowhawk, 300mm + 1.4x conv., f4, 90th, K200

Water rail, 800mm, f5.6, 60th, K200

79: Dog rose, 100mm macro, f6.7, 10th, K25

80: Toads, 200mm, f5.6, 250th, K200

Swans, 200mm, f8, 350th, K200

ACKNOWLEDGMENTS

Hidden Jewels would not have been published without the enthusiastic support and assistance of the following, to whom I owe a sizeable debt of gratitude: Eddie Howard, who inspired me to take up wildlife photography; Neil Randon, for the stylish design and maps; Janet Hickman, for meticulous editing; Dr Paul Krause, for helpful comments on content; Duncan Nowson and my fellow committee members of the Leatherhead & District Countryside Protection Society; and Cllr Kit Oliver, for writing the foreword.